San Diego
on my mind

Text by PETER JENSEN

Photography by STEPHEN SIMPSON

FALCON®

Design, typesetting, and other prepress work
by Falcon®, Helena, Montana.
Printed in Korea.

Library of Congress Number: 89-080767

ISBN 1-56044-392-8

Carlsbad flower fields

Beneath a dusky tent of oaks I roll my car to a stop, the engine quiet in the predawn hour. Only amber parking lights send a weak glow across the spiny leaves and dust covering a rural neighborhood street. I push the headlight knob on the dashboard all the way in and darkness comes down to meet the windshield—a darkness you don't expect to find close by the country's sixth-largest metropolis. A row of mailboxes, leaning arthritically against each other, proves that a few people live here on the flanks of this small San Diego mountain, but only a few. Their homes, once remote, are now adjacent to a parkland trailhead, and the mountain has become a popular destination for weekend hikers and rock climbers.

The stars are out, scratching bright paths across their inked bowl, but beneath the car's roof I see only the shapes of my camera bag and a small belt pack. I strap on the pack, leaving the pouch in front so I don't crush the fruit and crackers that will be my breakfast at sunrise. A sunrise is the best introduction any newcomer can have to San Diego, this natural and man-made wonder deep in the southwestern corner of the continental United States, bounded by ocean on one side, an international border on another, mountains and desert to the east, and the immense congregations of Los Angeles and Orange counties to the north. A sunrise is the simple beginning of a San Diego day that can become so varied with activities and possibilities as to be unforgettable—but also strangely indefinable.

I slide out of the car and feel the sixty-degree air draining off the slope above me. It moves—slides—under the covers of warmer, summery air coming off a mattress of dark roads and fields in a nearby valley. In a city where the wilderness of open ocean comes face to face with beaches crowded with houses, where one of the hottest, most formidable deserts on the globe lies just beyond a mountain range (yet within the same county as home gardens that nurture delicate orchids from Central American rain forests), one needs the constant of a sunrise to start understanding the place. It is a reminder to a modern San Diegan that no matter how varied his or her city and county become, how changeable the landscape is in its reliance on imported water and plants from around the world, this is still a place of sere, harsh natural beauty that makes everything else seem impermanent.

This is the day's true beginning: first light on Mt. Woodson, a boulder-pile sentinel that rises on some invisible line where San Diego's metropolis thins out in its spread eastward and the backcountry begins. It is the only mountain I know that I can climb in the dark—the trail is a still-serviceable jeep road up to an abandoned fire lookout—and I walk quickly against the incline, my heart noisy, my flashlight's beam flicking ahead of my feet only when I need it.

To the east the sky is lightening, going from black to a deep purple curtain that pulls at the stars, netting them with its growing light. Most of the rocks around me are cut by deep fissures—cracked eggs in a geologic nest that look like half of them might tumble into the valley, orphaned by a strong earthquake.

At 32 degrees 39.9'N, 117 degrees 14.5'W—far to the west of me on Point Loma—the lighthouse must be sending its last signals from a headland that Juan Rodriguez Cabrillo sailed his small bark past in 1542—and into a calm, sheltering bay. This is first light: the signal for bees swarming in the eave of the old redwood Grossmont Inn to start their morning fighter-pilot runs, cold power lines to stretch and warm and shake off the dew along the road to Santa Ysabel, and surfers to turtle offshore, belly down, head up, into the green-glass water that's building today with a south swell.

I step onto a cluster of boulders, pull the camera out,

Stripes at the beach

and prop it on a flat spot for a time exposure. The shutter sounds harsh, predatory, as I click off a frame every few minutes while the sky blushes brighter and brighter. Then the sun breaks free in a sharp angle between two peaks on the Laguna crest.

I can almost feel the city warming behind me, hear a few engines start in the distant valley, and, for the first time that morning, I feel that I'm not alone.

I have another thought, this one less explicable. Although surrounded by people, attractions, and the beauty of San Diego's place and climate, the city still eludes me, defying specifics. It is a place that stays on your mind, but not *of* any mind that wants to categorize, size up, pin down, and move on.

You find San Diego in waves, sunrises, sunsets, old houses with birdbaths, or papery hibiscus flowers against white walls. Perhaps you find it in the little parallel sand ripples on the sea bottom that guide you along shore as you swim beyond the break for a half mile or more.

San Diego's first light may come over the Laguna crest, but life here begins close to The Edge. Give visitors to San Diego one week— one glorious week of perfect weather—and they may do nothing but go to this Edge, this place of sand and rock.

Thirty years after first visiting San Diego as a child, I return to live in a small coastal town. The low heart murmur of waves bringing in their clouds of sand to the Del Mar beach comes through the bedroom window I leave open all year. The ocean, despite being several hundred yards away down the bluff and hiding at the foot of deeply veined cliffs, can be heard as easily as an Iowa farmer listens to a strange car pull into his driveway a quarter mile away.

Not long after arriving, my wife and I meet photographer Stephen Simpson on the doorstep of one of the city's most remarkable houses: the "Taj." A landmark from the days when almost no houses hung off the hillside above La Jolla Shores, the Taj looks like a small, white temple with Hershey Kiss-shaped topknots on its domes. We stand in a courtyard surrounded by a circle of thin, carved columns, then step inside and up a narrow, curving stairway into the main tower where Simpson lives and works. It is a circular room, a ring of glass that gathers the view from La Jolla Cove to the cliffs of Torrey Pines.

Simpson is soft-spoken, clean shaven, with eyes the color of the ocean on a day when

The setting sun highlights a cruise ship

the sun's out and there's barely a degree of humidity in the air. They're set in a permanent squint, probably from looking out to sea too much.

"I never have believed I live here," Simpson says. "It won't last forever, and I already know it may be the most unusual place I'll ever call home."

There's a door to a balcony, and we step out into the breeze. The rooftops below fight for space amidst the crowns of old trees shading a neighborhood that's been one of the city's most desirable addresses for the last sixty years.

"Do you go down to the beach often?"

"Never enough."

The white-washed plaster leaves a mark on our shoulders when we lean against the walls of the Taj's dome. We spend an hour just looking at the intense blue of deep water where a submarine canyon swings unusually close to shore.

The next week has a low tide early in the morning, and three of us—Steve Simpson, my wife Janeen, and I—go down to the beach again to take photographs and hike to the La Jolla Caves, which are usually all but inaccessible except by rubber raft or swimming.

From the Marine Room, a restaurant built in La Jolla Shores on a curving concrete foundation that throws the waves back out to sea, we walk down a narrow beach access way between buildings, the bottom steps strewn with kelp. No waves gnaw at the aquarium-thick picture windows of the Marine Room today, where a diner once said, "Waiter, please bring me a higher table!" What small waves there are have retreated almost one hundred yards out, exposing eel grass-covered molars of black, soft rock that normally lurk a few feet under the surf.

Once, a storm combined with high tides sent waves through the dining room; the windows didn't hold. Furniture sloshed around in waist deep water and the Marine Room was not unlike the Titanic going under for the last time. But the glass was replaced and bulwarks strengthened, ready for the next luck-of-the-draw combination of tide and storm.

San Diegans who live on the coast have seen the Pacific rear up and crash right through their living rooms, but they soon rebuild sea walls, fashion temporary plywood covers for plate glass windows, and return to living. It's a fatalistic—and steep—price to pay for building at the sand's edge, but it continues to be a price worth paying.

Either that, or they've just bought the house and don't know that the Pacific—the "peaceful" sea—can be so cantankerous.

We walk down the coast, Steve keeping his camera bag over one shoulder and slung to the small of his back for balance. I look up only when I stop walking, complaining that there's a sprained ankle waiting here for one of us. Simpson shrugs as if to say, "When you're carrying a bunch of expensive glass over your shoulder, you don't slip."

The water, the land, and all creatures—from a large sea slug trapped in a tidepool to the armies of nimble crabs that dash under rocks as we approach—are protected here. Even big waves aren't welcome once we move further into the bend of the coastline. Alligator Head near the Cove protects this feminine curve of coast shaped like a waistline above a hip, until the sea seems more like a lake than the end destination of waves several thousand miles in the building.

A squadron of brown pelicans assembles in flight above the cliffs, then straggles off toward us, flying just above the timid waves, wing feathers spread like fingers. At rest, these birds are odd statues with woeful, downcast beaks, knobby heads, and squat bodies. In flight they're transformed. Wings stretch out and out in seraphim grace, and their glide-wingbeat-glide flight is the most elegant dance on the coastline. Once endangered, the brown pelican has made such a strong comeback that the species seems almost commonplace along this shore.

The sea continues to carve caves into these cliffs, searching out cracks and fissures in the rock caused by earthquake action over the millenia. Some are only large enough to crouch in, their floors filled with cobblestones, but ahead of us we can see a line of shadowy, peak-roofed openings, each over twenty feet tall. Like mourning, long-dressed ladies, these dark shapes stroll beneath a tree-fringed stretch of La Jolla called Coast Walk.

If we were true La Jollans, members of a tribe that lived here year-round until the early 1800s, we would be gathering urchins and mussels for lunch, our bare feet inured to the rocks, sand, and broken shells. Once, while talking to a La Jolla lifeguard, I was asked if I'd like to see some finds from the diving he'd done at another La Jolla beach on his days off. We walked to a small apartment nearby and there, resting heavily on the shelves like Noguchi sculptures, were several Indian grinding stones and pestles.

"I found these in about 20 feet of water, well offshore and outside of the Preserve," he says, and after a moment adds, "There may be hundreds out there. I'm not sure why. Maybe that was the actual coastline several hundred years ago. Or maybe these were old and just discarded from canoes—a sort of submarine city dump. They might even have been some sort of offering to a continued life of good fishing and hunting."

The three of us are getting closer to the caves. Only the first four are accessible without a swim;

Pygmy chimpanzee at the San Diego Zoo

the others are off-limits not only because of their surging front doors but the danger of being caught deep inside by a rogue wave or rising tide.

Further down toward the Cove is The Hole, which, according to a story in the *La Jolla Light,* lifeguard Ron Trenton feels is "one of the few places on this coast that really casts fear into the hearts of guards. There's just no escape. I know. On January 29, 1976—I'll always remember that—I went in after a guy that had been whale watching from a raft." The two of them were thrown against a rock by a huge wave, permanently damaging Trenton's back.

We enter the first low opening and scramble back into the gloom. Within thirty feet the ocean seems far away, the light dim. Crouching now, we walk another twenty feet beneath the cliff where we find an opening to another cave that leads back out to sea. Here water, probably runoff from the lawns of La Jolla houses up on the flanks of Mt. Soledad, has formed a slick bacon of mineral deposits. We head back out to light.

The big cave is like a gramophone, gathering sound from off the ocean and playing it back. After an hour of listening, watching the birds wheel overhead, and crawling into another double cave, we head back. The water is up to the top of some of our foothold rocks, but not enough to worry. Even wet feet are worth the trouble of occasionally seeing a stretch of coast not stamped with bright towels and picnic coolers.

Encinitas boat houses

Windsurfing on Mission Bay

" In this neighborhood there are places of extraordinary fertility. Cultivation has always been by irrigation, and the soil seems to require only water to produce vigorously. Among the arid, brush-covered hills south of San Diego we found little valleys converted by a single spring into crowded gardens, where pears, peaches, quinces, pomegranates, grapes, olives, and other fruits grew luxuriantly together, the little stream acting upon them like a principle of life. "

John C. Frémont,
Memoirs

Bougainvillea

Blooming bougainvillea in Presidio Park

Evening on San Diego Bay

The James R. Mills Building and clock tower

Architect Rob Wellington Quigley's avant-garde downtown house

Rancho Santa Fe

Equestrian event at the Fairbanks Ranch during the 1984 Olympics

La Costa Hotel and Spa

Torrey Pines State Beach

“ *I wish we could go by the shore, Majella. It is beautiful there. When it is still, the waves come as gently to the land as if they were in play; and you can ride along with your horse's feet in the water, and the green cliffs almost over your head; and the air off the water is like wine in one's head.* ”

Helen Hunt Jackson,
Ramona

A Torrey pine at Torrey Pines State Reserve

Heavy dew on a golf course at Rancho Santa Fe

The 16th hole at Torrey Pines Golf Course

66 *I walked over to the edge of the cliff and listened to the sound of the surf. I couldn't see anything but the occasional gleam of a wave breaking out beyond the cove. In the cove the waves don't break, they slide in politely, like floorwalkers. There would be a bright moon later, but it hadn't checked in yet.* 99

Raymond Chandler,
Playback

Horton Plaza in downtown San Diego

Grand opening at Horton Plaza

The Half-notes entertaining at Horton Plaza

Deco diner

" *Downtown's motto ought to be 'Under Construction.' I had a visitor from the East Coast in my office recently and, seeing the steel rising for a new building, he asked me what it was. I had to confess, 'I don't know, it wasn't there yesterday.'* **"**

Lee Grissom,
Greater San Diego Chamber of Commerce

Having fun in the Gaslamp Quarter

Gaslamp Quarter's nostalgic streetlights

Dining in the Gaslamp Quarter

The Lewis Bank of Commerce in the heart of the Gaslamp Quarter

The Star of India

Yacht racing on San Diego Bay

Hoisting sails on the Star of India

> **" *Thus did we arrive, all in good health, happy and contented, at the famous and very desireable port of San Diego. God be praised.* "**
>
> Junipero Serra

The Fountain of Two Oceans in the First Interstate Plaza

Windsurfers on the San Diego waterfront

Open house on a Navy destroyer at Broadway Pier

A sailboat in the Christmas Parade of Lights on San Diego Bay

San Diego—Coronado Bay Bridge

Ferryboat Berkeley at sunset

End of G Street at dusk

Junipero Serra Museum in Presidio Park

San Diego—Coronado Bay Bridge

Yachts at Harbor Island

“ One gets the feel of the city best near sunset on a bright, warm day, standing atop Point Loma. The boot-shaped main harbor, inky velvet at twilight, becomes the main street of the city. It glows red, white and blue in the lights of the sky line and those of descending seaplanes or warships and yachts at anchor. The ocean and setting sun are the backdrop to the west. To the east, sometimes capped with snow, the Laguna Mountains of the coastal range stand sentinel. ”

Neil Morgan,
Westward Tilt

29

Los Charros in Old Town

Mexican dancers in Old Town during Cinco de Mayo

A Mexican dancer, Old Town

Coronado Beach in front of Hotel del Coronado

Hotel del Coronado

At night . . . when the tide is out the sand of my shoreline becomes snow, ankle-deep. My boots sink into it making the crunch-crunch-crunch sound so familiar in Dakota or Montana during winters. I could be there, and my desolate beach could be a January prairie. For even on the darkest nights, nights when there is no moon and when the stars are blurred, the shoreline maintains that certain radiance so common with snow. This radiance frightens the night away. Night may hover but may not land, and these are the hours to go walking, if walk one will.

Max Miller,
I Cover The Waterfront

Evening at Torrey Pines State Beach

Soaring over Torrey Pines State Beach

Making giant bubbles at Mission Bay

a temperate place

Where one stretch of coast in San Diego County may be wild, in or under water, another entirely different strand is sure to be close by, usually a carpet of sand overlooked by houses. Where one Edge is sudden, steep, eaten by landslides that drop silently to the beach during storms, the other is a low sea wall topped with a portable stereo tape machine, a place where a volleyball arcs lazily back and forth and a thousand bicyclists stream along a path barely wide enough for a car—if cars were allowed.

This is the San Diego that the bulk of the county's population lives in. Call it the coastal zone, the place people go when they want to sit, surf, swim, play, or just escape the heat of inland valleys. It's found the entire length of San Diego County. The influence of marine air extends inland as much as 15 to 20 miles, depending on gaps in the coastal mountains and mesas, so the definition of this zone can be almost as broad as you like. One thing is definite: this is a user-friendly part of San Diego, beginning with the closest place to sleep near waves and moving east to the mountains that wall out the desert.

"I could see it comin," Old Joe says, as he rears back from the railing at Crystal Pier in Pacific Beach and looks toward the horizon, as if it was out there once again. A few tufts of white hair stick out from beneath his old Greek fisherman's cap, and stubble covers his wrinkled chin.

"We'd been rockin' and rollin' all morning as them big storm waves hit the pier, but this one was bigger than the rest. I was out toward the end when the wave punched up, just like a boxer." With his fist, the one not holding a pole, Joe (no one knows his last name) takes a Popeye swing for emphasis, then drapes a blue-veined hand over his ample belly—his "Milwaukee goiter" as he calls it.

"It knocked a plank loose and hit me right here. Put the stuffing right out of me, I tell you."

Just as the ocean isn't kind to San Diego's cliffs or coastline houses, it tortures and tears at piers like Crystal. Still, the mussel-cloaked pilings stand up for decades, the only way to get out over the water except by boat. Even the section of Crystal Pier more toward the shore is covered with small motel rooms, each a testament to the advertising slogan "Sleep over the waves!"

I met the manager once and asked him what it was like. "Real nice," he said, "but sometimes the dresser's moved out from the far wall when you wake up, or the bed starts walking toward the middle of the room."

In San Diego the urge to get close to the water doesn't stop at building houses or spending your summers over a rocking sea to escape Arizona's heat or Michigan's humidity. *Sports Illustrated* once called this "Sports Town U.S.A." and added that it was all but impossible to stand anywhere, turn 360 degrees, and not see several sports taking place at once.

This applies, of course, to anything from kite flying to Olympic training in cycling and sailing. At times, it even applies to a strange sport called Over The Line, or OTL as the clannish members of the Old Mission Beach Athletic Club call it for short. In the true spirit of makeshift beach minimalism, OTL is softball played with no base runners, no pitchers, and no gloves. It makes about as much sense as cricket, but the uniforms are cheaper—everyone,

View from the 23rd floor of the Meridian

men's and women's teams, wears swimsuits.

Hitters stand at the point of a triangle formed in the sand with ropes, and hit a softball tossed gently into the air by a teammate kneeling only a few feet away to the side. The hit must be "over the line"—a rope stretched at right angles to the hitter about the same distance out as a pitcher's mound in standard baseball (the actual distance was determined by simply counting twenty steps taken by one of the sport's founders).

If the ball drops to the sand without being caught by the other team (and there are only three to a side), score it a run. Caught, and the hitter's out. Over everyone's head: home run. It's difficult to cover the field, especially when expert hitters send clothesline drives into the sand just past the line—hits so hot to handle that your hands feel like hamburger after a few games.

Somehow, in ways unknown to anyone but OTL fanatics, this sport has become San Diego's biggest beach event of the year—a sort of Super Bowl each July of sand and beer. Tens of thousands of sunburnt spectators and participants, in various stages of undress, swarm over Fiesta Island, a barren patch of sand and grass surrounded by Mission Bay. By tradition, team names are always off-color enough to guarantee unprintability in the local press, adding to the cachet of something that has half of San Diego wondering "What the hell do they do out there?"

In North County, it's 6:00 a.m. as John Armstrong, Tim Kelly, Doug Goodell, and Tom Close gather in Armstrong's driveway in Del Mar beneath three ornamental fig trees, their leaves wet with morning fog. Close is a pilot, Goodell a schoolteacher, Kelly an engineer, and Armstrong a hospital administrator, and they all live in houses scattered up a hillside formed when ancient sandstone formations tilted skyward along the coast. Four of thousands of bicyclists in San Diego, they're out for their usual morning ride, perhaps inland as far as Escondido and Spook Canyon, a narrow two-lane road back to the coast through a rural valley, or northward along the coast roads to Oceanside and the marine base.

This morning I join them, pedaling through the San Dieguito River Valley eastward toward the eucalyptus-covered hills of Rancho Santa Fe, one of the most exclusive communities in the country. Armstrong looks back over his left shoulder as I begin to fall behind and shouts, "Try getting behind me and drafting! Put your front wheel just an inch or two from mine."

Like a multilegged insect in bright elastic pants and tight nylon shirts (all in neon-lipstick colors so obnoxious that cars can't help but see us), we trail each other over the hills. Now and then the leader drops his left arm from the handle bar and points toward the ground as if to say "Broken glass!" We swerve as one. Finally it's my turn to lead. I pull in front of Armstrong and feel like I'm swimming through cotton candy. Almost immediately the added work of bucking a headwind slows down my legs, burns into the thighs, and I drop back and start praying for a flat tire.

You can get bored in San Diego near the coast. Everyone does after awhile. What draws you to The Edge also sends you rushing inland, fleeing the plastic thickets of signs and drive-up windows in some pockets of the beach cities, the headphoned roller skaters, the buffed body builders preening like birds in a Costeau documentary, the lost long-hairs wandering the coast twenty years after Peoples' Park in Berkeley, and the intermittent wet. The Big Wet.

It lays on your car in the morning, crawling into every crack in the paint until bubbles of rust bloom next to door handles, roof racks, and latches—a kind of topside rust instead of

Sea World's Christmas Tree of Lights

the running-board rust of the snow states. It comes with heavy, white, sound-muffling fog that rolls up the streets first in patches, then thick, blanket-like as the coastal areas of the city are tucked in beneath a cloud cover that doesn't break for most of May and June.

Some meteorologists call it the Catalina Eddy, a condition of marine-layer clouds caused by warm inland air masses and still-cool ocean waters, all of it stuck in a sort of cauldron formed by the bight in Southern California's coastline. San Diegans call it the June Gloom—a cruel irony of weather that drops on the coastline after several spring months of sparkling clear days and little rain.

No groundhog can expect to see his shadow in San Diego in June—unless he lives inland. The Other San Diego. The one the tourists never find because they're too busy driving to the edge of the continent.

San Diego is a series of mesas and canyons that look like a waffle bootprint stretching from the sea to about twenty miles inland, where mountains begin their slow rise to the Laguna crest above the desert. The land is unlike anything elsewhere in Southern California. It is like few places in the world.

These mesas and canyons continue to define the landscape despite the notions of skiploaders and bulldozers to rearrange anything that looks like it needs filling, or leveling any feature resembling a hill. Seen from the air, the neighborhoods above San Diego's largest watercourse, Mission Valley, spread in venular patterns along the canyon rims. Here backyard lawns give way to chaparral (and coyotes make quick work of unwary house pets out for a stroll in the evening). Planners call these canyons the "lungs of the city," and seen from two thousand feet through the ice-scratched plexiglass window of a Cessna Centurion they do look to me like bronchial branches stretching and narrowing, sometimes beset by an asphalt pneumonia, sometimes connecting, sometimes burned naked by wildfires, always widening until the final meeting with San Diego Bay, Mission Bay, or the open ocean.

"There were dairy farms here and here," a charter pilot yelled to me as she turned the plane over Mission Valley, now a kind of urban trough holding the final miles of Interstate 8, its flanks bristling with motels and hotels where tiki torches hooked to underground gas lines flicker around turquoise swimming pools. "We'd ride horses along the San Diego River

up toward Mission Gorge and the original dam built by the Padres. It's still there, but not much else."

Within a half mile of two interstates, Mission San Diego de Alcala ("Where California Began," and "The Dream of Father Junipero Serra," say the postcards) is a quiet remnant of San Diego's rough and often dangerous beginnings. One of the mission fathers was martyred by Indians incensed with their treatment at the hands of presidio soldiers. On summer nights the home-run roars from baseball crowds in Jack Murphy Stadium drift across Interstate 15 until they meet the plain, white adobe facade, mission yard, and parking lot, then wing on into the night with the ghost of Father Luis Jayme.

Inland summer days are hot—shimmering hot in the valley called El Cajon. Here San Diego can come closest to being like Los Angeles. The trapped valley air, pushed by ocean breezes against the mountains, eddies and cooks its ozone into a brown haze on some days. Still, the heat is a blessing for many residents, a reliable relief from coastal cloud covers that don't burn off until noon—if at all. Avocado trees crowd backyard fences, vegetable gardens produce corn by June, and some home orchards thrive enough in the frosty hollows to set stone fruits despite San Diego's mild winters.

Rancho Bernardo

An agave plant in front of Mission San Diego de Alcala

Early morning on Market Street

Flamingo at the San Diego Zoo

Thai visitors

Shamu performing at Sea World

Starfish in tide pool at Sea World

Double slices of watermelon for a happy picnicker

Showering at Pacific Beach

Sand sculpture at Pacific Beach

Fireworks over San Diego Bay

Centro Cultural de la Raza at Balboa Park

Renaissance Fair at Balboa Park

The Casa del Prado in Balboa Park

Aero-Space Museum

Hot-air balloons above Del Mar

Alcazar Gardens in Balboa Park

Lawn bowling at Balboa Park

Hibiscus

> 66 *Not since pagan veneration of the sacred oaks of Jupiter have trees received the honor that three generations of San Diegans have bestowed upon the eucalyptus variety. San Diegans planted olive trees by the hundreds, citrus trees by the thousands, and eucalyptus by the multi-million. Olive and citrus indeed contributed to bodily welfare, but the coming of the eucalyptus from Australia was, to many people, the long awaited Millenium—practically a supernatural beneficence to every area of life: economical, medicinal, and ethereal. Eucalyptus provided not only wonder wood and wonder drugs, but wonder miracles. Indeed, to many early Americans it was 'wunderbar'. . . .* 99

Leland G. Stanford,
Journal of San Diego History

Eucalyptus

Fountains in Balboa Park

San Diego Symphony

You can either work or you can have a good time but you can't do both. Well, San Diegans do both. These people have a good time. And they couldn't be more right. All work and no play not only makes Jack a dull boy, it means he doesn't live as long or contribute as much to society. San Diego is a monument to the other Jack.

Dr. Mark Shipman,
quoted in Sports Illustrated

The San Diego Convention Center capped by its rooftop "tents," with North Island across the harbor and Point Loma in the distance.

Watching the sunset at Mission Beach

Surfboards

Mission Beach

Catching a long ride

Skateboarders at Mission Beach

Roller coaster at Belmont Park, Mission Beach

"The Plunge" at Mission Beach

Belmont Park at Mission Beach

Go anywhere. Go up to Mount Soledad, down to the Embarcadero or out to Crystal Pier. Go anywhere in San Diego, anywhere, stop for a moment, make one complete 360-degree turn, and if you don't see at least two dozen people engaged in a minimum of three different sports, well, it's either four o'clock in the morning or you've taken the wrong turnoff and ended up in Tijuana.

Steve Cushman,
quoted in Sports Illustrated

Window washer at Mission Beach

Windsurfing on Mission Bay

San Diego Crew Classic at Mission Bay

Boardwalk on Mission Beach

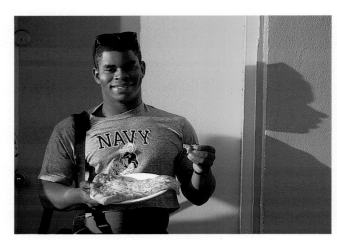

Pizza at the beach

A little lifeguard at La Jolla Shores

Stars & Stripes practicing for America's Cup

Sunset on Mission Beach

Seagulls

Sunset over La Jolla Shores

A kaleidoscope of color at the Del Mar Fair

California Theater neon

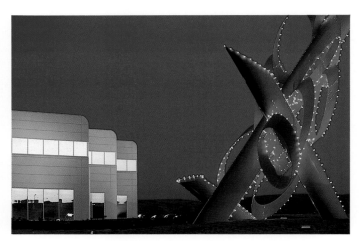

Naiman Tech Center

where mountains and desert meet

On the road to Potrero—one of the county's busiest and most winding rural roads —the bumper stickers proclaim, "Pray for me: I drive Highway 94." This is another side of San Diego County, on the rim between the desert and coast; a country that prefers fried catfish to Hobie Cats, and Jimmie trucks to anything with doors less than three feet off the ground.

I'm driving a carload of Boy Scouts to a camporee on the international border near the border town of Tecate, and the Kentucky Fried buckets of Spring Valley and Casa de Oro have given way to stacks of hay wrapped in blue tarps. A sign says, "15O ACRES 4 SALE $3,000 PER," and pretentious gates to empty land stand beside the roadway, the beginnings—or end—of someone's estate dreams. We pass Freezer Road in Morongo Valley; no script writer could make up names as good as these.

At the Dulzura Cafe we stop to stretch our legs beneath a Coors on Tap sign in the window. In the gas island, where the meters are long since stuck on forty-four cents for Regular Mohawk, a wooden wishing well has its sides cut out to reveal a greenish aquarium filled with lazily finning goldfish. Down the road a few dozen yards, a round plywood sign says, "YOU'VE JUST MISSED THE BEST FOOD AND THE COLDEST BEER IN TOWN."

There is a dust here that lies invisible, waiting for a foot or tire to kick it free. Then it rises in a brown plume behind cars that pull off onto the shoulder to let faster, impatient drivers pass—probably residents who know every curve and ride the slickers' rear bumpers, their front grills filling the rearview mirror, until the slowpokes get the point and pull over. No one honks. They just get close.

Where Cottonwood Creek comes close to the road, the marsh cane looks like wild corn. Sometimes there are houses, usually set in patches up near the top of hills without a tree around them. You see their match-stick gazebos, birdhouses for people and barbecues, sitting out on the edge of a barren field, taking in the view of the neighbors' houses and some blue jean-colored mountains.

How long can a road go double-yellow? Miles. And miles.

This is fire country, and the chaparral hills biologically expect a burn every decade or

Dulzura Cafe

two; the dormant seeds rely on heat to scar their tough jackets so they can sprout after a fall rain. Buckwheat lines the road cuts in brown clumps as if shotgunned across the rocky soil, and the smell of dry oaks fills some of the hollows to where it's like sticking your nose inside a tack shop piled with old leather and hay.

At Portrero we spend the night camped in a valley of oaks. The soft duff beneath our sleeping bags is about four inches thick and crawling with red ants, and any water spilled at the drinking fountains where we fill our cooking pots sinks into the thirsty ground. It may not be as postcard-beautiful as a redwood grove or a set of glacier-carved ledges beneath a waterfall, but the empty, dry land is still precious to those who use the county's backcountry. Although San Diego's growth pressures are intense, over forty percent of the county is still public land, from national forests down to pocket-size city parks.

These East County mountains along the border are the remnants of an ancient river bed so large (as one theory has it) that rocks the size of houses were tumbled smooth. The river wasn't located here, but was actually in what we today call Mexico—millions of years before the incredible drift northward of this continental plate. On the way home we pass an archipelago of black cattle standing fetlock deep in a sea of barley, and roadside signs that announce small enterprise: "PINE NUTS and NICE BUNNIES $5." A *charreada* ring stands empty near the road waiting for a Sunday Mexican-style rodeo full of silver saddles and stylish riding.

The break with the backcountry comes at the Sweetwater Bridge, a curious symbol of San Diego old and new. On one side, black girders stand with skeletal grace, the bridge preserved as a walkway and bike path. Next to it, a new concrete span, wide enough so no one will ever again have to slow down and pray they don't meet a semi coming the other way, looks like its engineers copied a steak and lobster hot tray.

In a doughnut shop I ask the cashier, a young woman with her hair tied back with a bandana and cowboy boots showing beneath a long apron, if business is good. "It's better," she says, "since they built some more houses. We're getting bigger, all right, but I'm not sure I like it."

Rams Hill Country Club, Borrego Springs

You look for places in San Diego that define the land and what it was. Perhaps they're hidden in Cuyamaca, with its feeling of Indian history. In the catacombs of the Museum of Natural History in Balboa Park, Director Doug Sharon slowly pulls out a heavy wooden drawer to reveal thousands of arrowheads, many of them gathered at an Indian "factory" ridge in what is now Cuyamaca Rancho State Park.

As a boy, I would have given anything to find one arrowhead—one! Today I think that if I happened on these delicate, sometimes translucent shards, I'd look but leave them, like the time my boys and I found pottery fragments against a blackened rock in Anza-Borrego. When someone tries to reconstruct what life was like on that site, that Blair Valley kitchen, I don't want to intervene.

Often the definition comes from history. The San Diego Historical Society's library in Balboa Park, and their emerging Museum of San Diego History, hold stories of San Diego that range from grim to amusing, like the time a rainmaker, furious at not being paid, "started" the Sweetwater River flood.

But out in the desert, the part of San Diego County that hides behind mountains (some of them laced with gold) that run parallel to the coastline about forty miles inland, you think mainly of heat, even in early May. From 1,500 feet atop the San Ysidro Mountains, the town of Borrego Springs looks like little more than whiskers on the desert's chin. Roads wrinkle their way across the valley floor, sometimes following a surveyor's transit line, sometimes not. Green swatches of irrigated land paint the checkerboard—grapefruit and palm groves, two golf courses, a school or two, and a circle in the center of town—but most of the land is a dusky, lion-fur color dotted by smoketree grays and ocotillo exclamation marks.

In a word, Borrego Springs is *quiet*. This desert town only ninety miles from San Diego has a feel to it much as Palm Springs must have had before the days of golf tournaments, tramways, and watering holes surrounded by stretch limos. You can imagine that you drove over from San Diego in a 1940 Packard, with Dorsey swinging on the radio until you lost him behind the last ridge. The nation's largest state park—Anza-Borrego Desert State Park—is here. With square mileage almost equal to some states, it surrounds the town with an emptiness that swallows visitors.

It's before 10 a.m., but already the mercury

reads eighty-five degrees on this spring day as we pull into the gravel parking lot of the park's visitor center. There are six of us, and we shoulder backpacks heavy with almost three gallons of water each for the short hike into Hellhole Canyon. One night is all we'll spend—water for two would simply weigh too much for pleasure.

We follow a wash in a southwestern direction from the visitor center, feeling the gentle elevation gain, as the air temperature warms to ninety-five degrees. I fold a bandana with the point inside, knot it across my forehead, and pour water on my head. The bandana catches the runoff and I begin to cool down. It may be one of the last weekends we can safely hike in the desert until late next fall, and we know we should have started earlier. Still, there are only a few miles to go to where the water springs free of the canyon's rocky "V" and falls in one high, but weak, waterfall through a wall of ferns.

Ed Mirsky, a biology teacher from the Coronado school system, stops often to listen for birds that are still out in the rising heat. We cross a dry wash, and an electronic-sounding chirp begins repeating in the air over our head.

"There's a Costa's hummingbird 'displaying'," says Mirsky, and we follow his line of sight until we see a tiny speck flying high-speed vertical loop-the-loops near a rock outcropping. To Mirsky and other naturalists, the desert is a constant fugue of sounds that otherwise seem lost amidst the noise of boots crunching across decomposed granite, the scrape of a walking stick over rock, and one's constant sucking at a plastic water bottle.

We set camp on an open sandy shelf well above the wash, and tie parabolic tarps between low, thorny shrubs to create some shade. Here we'll sit until late afternoon, missing the anvil of midday, then hike the last mile up to the waterfall and back at dusk.

"This camping isn't for everyone," one of us says, wondering if it's for us, either. But we're glad the visitor center is well behind us, and feel a certain satisfaction in not diving into a swimming pool to end the day.

Even the next morning, as we return to the visitor center, then take a short day hike up Palm Canyon for a swim in a rocky grotto, we feel apart from Borrego Springs and San Diego, sympathetic, at least, to the rare bighorn sheep and their quiet, ghost-like lives amid the rocks.

Fall colors in Penasquitos

Cabrillo National Monument on Point Loma

Fort Rosecrans National Cemetery

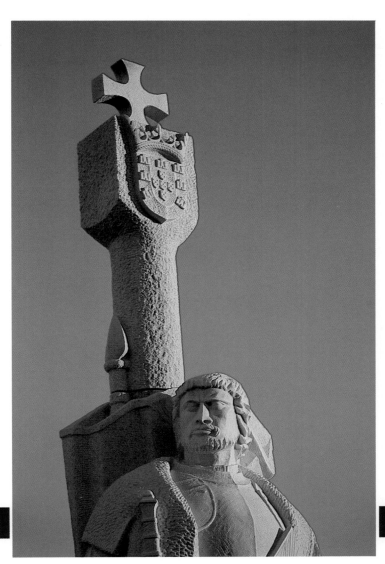

Cabrillo National Monument

Iris

Moon rising over San Diego

Downtown San Diego at night

Normal Heights downtown district

Loma Theater

El Cajon Boulevard

Downtown Hillcrest

San Diego County Administration Building along the Embarcadero

Fishing boat at the G Street Pier

Fishing nets

A successful lobster fisherman off Point Loma

Reliving the 1950s at the Corvette Diner

Interstates 8 and 805 interchange in Mission Valley

Central University Library, University of California at San Diego

“ *We will be looking into the most elementary processes of life and for the way in which basic structures relate to and control one another to make a complete living being, from the brain down. The institution will be best expressed by the kinds of people who ask new questions.* ”

Jonas Salk

Salk Institute

Coastline along the Torrey Pines State Reserve

Tidal caves at La Jolla

La Valencia Hotel in La Jolla

Colonial Inn in La Jolla

Wall Street Plaza, La Jolla

Palms line Coast Boulevard in La Jolla

La Jolla cove

Scuba divers

Tide pools at La Jolla

La Jolla Shores

Sunbathing in La Jolla cove

Relaxing at Windansea Beach

Boogie boarders at Windansea Beach

Beach volleyball at Mission Bay

Strolling at Del Mar

Purple iceplant along the La Jolla coast

Dusk at La Jolla

La Jolla is a bit of sea coast of many moods and manners, sometimes sparkling, crisp, buoyant; again despondent, troubled, morose; at intervals, tumultuous, defiant, angry but the dominant mood is soothing, restful and comforting.

San Diego Union,
January 1, 1923

Bicyclists' sunset at La Jolla

Oceanside Pier

The Palomar Observatory

Highway 79 near Lake Cuyamaca

Lazy days at McClintock Saddle Works

Shopping on the Main Street of Ramona

Oak leaves above Cuyamaca Lake

Sunset behind a backcountry oak

" *This is no boom based on wheat deals, or pork corners, or other devices of man. It is based on the simple fact that hereabouts the good Lord has created conditions of climate and health and beauty such as can be found nowhere else in this or any land.* *"*

Real-estate promotion

"Golden Triangle" 1983

"Golden Triangle" 1989

a "new town" still new

San Diegans expect things that, in many other parts of the country, are only vague wishes.

They expect good weather, weather so stable that it easily attracts the very industry that depends on clear skies and light winds: aeronautics. The first sea plane took off from San Diego Harbor, John J. Montgomery launched man's first controlled, winged flight off a hillside above the Otay Valley in 1883 (long before the Wright Brothers' powered flight), and even Lindbergh came to San Diego to have some of the country's best engineers build *Spirit of St. Louis.* Here, over the years, the top men in flight have gathered, and they came first for the weather.

San Diegans expect to be accepted, even as newcomers. Over a million people have arrived in the last two decades; even more going back to the last world war. "I saw it as a G.I. on my way to the Pacific," is what men and their families, now in their 60s and 70s, remember first about San Diego. This needs to be a friendly place—where people talk in supermarket lines and expect to see familiar faces in restaurants and theaters—because it lacks the small town patterns and family ties of the Midwest, New England, or the South.

San Diegans expect to be shocked by the prices of land and housing, but never outraged. There is an exponential logic to San Diego prices, and it's based on supply and demand. Most San Diegans are fatalists, realizing that the same urge that drove them to emigrate to this southwest corner will continue to pull in new residents. And prices will continue to rise.

Most of all, they expect to avoid all the problems that have beset their neighbor Los Angeles to the north. If they wanted Los Angeles, they would have moved *there.*

Looking down on the Emerald City of Balboa Park as I ride in a small interstate commercial jet making its final approach to Lindbergh field, I see the fantasy of San Diego's churrigueresque California Tower and museums, a movie-set quality created by the Panama-California Exposition of 1915-1916 in which park visitors still promenade along a Spanish street called El Prado.

The bay has lost its borders in a welter of breakwaters, ship repair yards, marinas, and naval bases, but retains its essential sheltering shape—an almost secret place guarded by the encircling arm of Point Loma.

We lurch down. The runway is short and the engines roar in protest as the pilot brakes fast. We've just landed in one of the few airports in the world located in the middle of a major city. I'll barely have time to lean back in my cab seat before I'm downtown.

Here change is most obvious. This place once called New Town by founder Alonzo Horton has sent dozens of buildings and a huge new convention center into the skyline in the 1980s, shaking off the doldrums of the previous two decades, when it was feared that downtown had been permanently abandoned by shoppers (and even office workers) during the march to the suburbs and the urbanization of Mission Valley.

Downtown has been reborn as the center of a city almost three hundred square miles in size: a new "New Town" set in a county of over 4,258 square miles of land. It's about seventy miles from the northern border in San Clemente to the San Ysidro border crossing into Tijuana—and a simple step through a metal gate into another culture that seems paradoxically to be familiar and alien at the same time. From the beaches, you drive inland eighty miles to the Imperial County line.

If it is nothing else, San Diego County is big,

Reflections of change

big enough to finally need this true center.

But it is much more—a natural and artificial world so varied that residents sometimes express the philosophy, "Why leave? Millions of people are traveling from around the country—and the world—to get *here* for their vacations."

On a crisp morning in downtown San Diego, Armand Viora is jangling his key ring outside the door to his small locksmith shop, a ritual he has performed almost every workday morning for the last sixty-one years. Above his blue-roofed shop, which looks like a tiny streetcar attached to the side of the building, the morning sun slants down F Street and warms the Victorian-era brick arches of the nearby Keating Building.

"I've never seen downtown change as much as it has in the last five years," says Viora as he slides open a window facing the street, flips over the CLOSED sign, and takes his seat on a high stool—creakily now, for his legs just aren't what they used to be when he spent his weekends riding the mountain trails to his cabin up near Julian.

Armand Viora is one of San Diego's longest-tenured observers—a man who counts as friends everyone from bank presidents to sailors who've lost the keys to their lockers. Since 1928 he's occupied this corner and seen it go from good, to bad, to worse, and back again (but not all the way yet).

For years I had my office in the building above him, and from the fourth floor I looked down on what is called the Gaslamp District—a few square blocks of Victorian buildings that somehow avoided the wrecker's ball over the last three or four decades of decline until downtown suddenly became a hot property again with the opening of Horton Plaza. Viora and I would talk as I left for lunch, or came back from getting a cup of coffee around the corner. I'd lean my elbows on the worn,

nubby rubber mat he keeps on his glass case full of antique and collectors' item keys, while he'd peer out from under the brim of his ever-present cap through metal-rimmed bifocals.

"It's something," says Armand. "I guess no one got around to telling San Diego about hard times."

Indeed, New Town businessmen in the 1870s couldn't get over the amount of dust and fleas this city could produce. There were several bust times, and even a *Time* magazine cover that announced "Bust Town U.S.A." as San Diego geared down after the war—a time when as many as thirty thousand workers had riveted together bombers in one factory. Today their counterparts, more often white-collared in a "clean industry" world of finance, research, and academia, lunch at outdoor tables in restored brick warehouses, sip beer in new microbreweries, and gather at sundown in restaurants overlooking a bay where towering aircraft carriers jostle with fleets of spinnakered sailboats.

Within walking distance of downtown, Balboa Park stretches its Persian carpet across the "uptown" neighborhoods. One of the great city parks in America, it owes its Andalusian look to the great Panama-California Exposition and the index finger of President Woodrow Wilson, who pushed a button to illuminate the grounds at midnight, January 1, 1915. I walk through the park on a Saturday, beginning at the Laurel Street entrance, crossing the graceful arches of a massive bridge above State Highway 163 in the canyon below (if highways can be beautiful, this, with its median row of California sycamores, is surely one of the prettiest). The Prado is a hive of activity, from the Museum of Man on the west to a great, gushing fountain in the east that's easily seen from the air. Other museums (art, photography, history, science, space, natural history and even one of the world's largest model railroad layouts) occupy the restored or rebuilt exposition buildings, and most have been completely rebuilt. Another aerospace museum is nearby, as is a car museum.

But the crown of the park is worn by its zoo—world-famous not only for its zoological collection but its botanic setting, where animals seem less in enclosures or cages than in Rousseau paintings complete with clouds of mist along a "Tiger River." I sit near the entrance,

Mariachis perform for a sales opening

where the flamingos strut about in a pink cloud, and watch the humanity tugged through these gates. Here the world meets San Diego, and San Diego mirrors back the very world these visitors are in danger of losing.

Before I leave, I stop by the fountain to watch a juggler riding a unicycle fifteen feet tall. I don't stay long enough to see how he gets down. Far more improbable are the forests of mature trees that cover the park's grounds, most of them planted by one woman horticulturist: Kate Sessions. Responsible for thousands of San Diego's finest trees throughout the city, Sessions, the "Mother of Balboa Park," operated nurseries, established botanical enclaves, and landscaped private homes from the 1880s on. Seeing her finest work here in the park, it is sometimes difficult to visualize San Diego as a mostly-treeless, chaparral landscape.

Nearby, in Mission Hills, Hillcrest, Golden Hills, and all along the mesas north and east of downtown, the great neighborhoods of San Diego echo this botanical ethic of exoticness and vibrant color. Here, too, flowered the most humane form of architecture to seed itself in Southern California: the bungalow court, where small housing units cluster around a central, landscaped court.

Today residents still shop at small markets, sip espresso at sidewalk cafes, prowl small antique and book shops, and take walks in the evening along sidewalks that bear contractor stamps from the early 1900s. It is a San Diego of a different time, and somehow it seems sorely missed. Yet one element of deja vu from this time and place has taken the city's imagination anew. Trolleys now run from downtown to the international border, and east as far as El Cajon. The neighborhoods are being reunited once again.

Talk with San Diegans about their city and you'll almost always get a short pause before they answer the question, "What makes San Diego... San Diego?" At breakfast one day in an uptown, jam-packed coffee shop that's an early-morning tradition (where the coffee always comes as soon as your cup is empty, and the biscuits are warm, flour-dusted pillows), a prominent physician took that usual pause and said, "It's a winter day, because there's no other winter day in the world like one in San Diego. How many places do you know that have a dry, mild climate next to a warm—but not tropical—sea? With a desert not more than sixty miles away over a range of beautiful mountains where you can ski-tour in the winter? Give me a winter day when the mountains are a cool blue, and the Coronado Islands look like Bora Bora out there—here I'll be, running along the beach with my shirt off."

San Diego's regional quality doesn't come entirely from climate, though, explains Hamilton Marston, a now-retired merchant (the Marston family department store business, now sold, dated back to the 1870s). Marston observes San Diego's growth with a keen eye, even personally commissioning a planning analysis of the region ten years ago. He addressed the question as he sat in the sun porch of his turn-of-the-century home designed by Irving Gill, San Diego's internationally known architect and one of the father's of American modernism.

Marston feels that "two things play a major role in San Diego's future. First, Camp Pendleton, the huge marine training base at the north edge of our county, buffers us from Los Angeles—Orange County growth. Second, Tijuana is now larger than San Diego, and San Diego is one of the ten largest metropolitan areas in the United States. We are inexorably linked to the border. We can't ignore the fact that we are, in a sense, joint tenants; sharing adjacent land masses and the same drainage basin and air basin."

"I know what it is about San Diego," Armand Viora says at the end of one day as he flips his sign over and pulls the door shut behind him. I'd caught him at closing—just in time for him to grind a copy of my front door key to give to houseguests who'd be spending all next week at my house (another side effect of living in a place with great winter weather).

Despite watching it all downtown—the homelessness, the sad, slow dance of drink, and the peep show era of San Diego's rowdy sailor-town past—Viora smiled and continued, "It's the people, They're friendly here. They love the place. They're just darned happy to be here, thankful that they're this lucky."

He tucked his keys into baggy khaki pants and walked slowly up Fifth Avenue just as the clusters of gaslamps—electric now—glowed to life.

Omni Hotel

Saddle bronc riding at the Lakeside Rodeo

Indian dancers at Balboa Park

Galloping on the mesa off Carmel Valley Road

Horseback riders in Carmel Valley

Lake Henshaw

A great catch

A snowy scene along Sunrise Highway in the Laguna Mountains

Evening view from Stonewall Peak

Climbing Stonewall Peak

Spring wildflowers

" We get seasons here. May and June are our cloudy months. "

Anonymous

Roadside camping outside Borrego Springs

" . . . the mountains of Borrego Badlands look as if they had been brought and piled up there, like the sweepings of the world. "

Padre Pedro Font,
Anza Expedition (1775-1776)

Ocotillo cactus at Font's Point

Moon rising over the Borrego Badlands

A hotel in the mountain community of Julian

Julian-made cider

Mom's Pie Shop

Kitchen at Mom's Pie Shop

The Tijuana Cultural Center

Photographer's stand in Tijuana

Paper flower seller

Jai Alai Palace in Tijuana

San Diego Convention Center

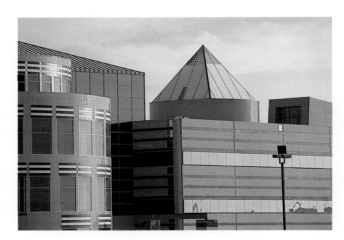

San Diego Design Center

UCSD Price Center

Life Flight helicopter at UCSD Medical Center

Walk like an Egyptian on Point Loma

Running through the warm dusk

Palm trees at West Mission Bay

about the author

Peter Jensen grew up in the San Francisco Bay Area, graduated from the University of Pacific, and began his writing career with *Sunset* magazine for nine years. For the last decade he has been Editor of *San Diego Home/Garden* magazine, an award-winning regional publication. His previous books include *California, The Coast of Oregon, San Diego, Yosemite—Shrine of the Sierra,* and *The West.* Since moving to San Diego in 1970, Jensen has lived in Del Mar with his wife and two children.

about the photographer

Stephen Simpson has been a resident of San Diego for seventeen years and a corporate/commerical photographer for the past ten years. A graduate of San Diego State with degrees in English, religious studies, and philosophy, he finds San Diego a perfect blend of urban and outdoor life. His photographs have appeared in *San Diego Magazine, San Diego Home/Garden, Architectural Record,* and other magazines. *San Diego on my Mind* is Simpson's first book.

acknowledgments

The publishers gratefully acknowledge permission to reprint the following material:

Page 17 from *Playback* by Raymond Chandler. Copyright © 1958 by the estate of Raymond Chandler.

Page 29 from *Westward Tilt* by Neil Morgan. Copyright © 1963 by Neil Morgan. Reprinted by permission of Random House, Inc.

Page 33 from *I Cover the Waterfront* by Max Miller. Copyright © 1932 by E.P. Dutton, Inc.

Page 51 from "San Diego's Eucalyptus Bubble," by Leland G. Stanford in *Journal of San Diego History,* Fall 1970. Reprinted by permission of the San Diego Historical Society.

Pages 53 and 62 reprinted courtesy of *Sports Illustrated,* from the December 25 - January 1, 1979, issue. Copyright © 1978-79, Time, Inc. "Sports Town, U.S.A. It's San Diego," by Ray Kennedy. All rights reserved.

Rocks on La Jolla beach

A sunset silhouette